CENTER FOR INTERNATIONAL SYSTEMS RESEARCH

OCCASIONAL PAPERS

NUMBER 2

SOME CAUSES OF

ORGANIZATIONAL INEFFECTIVENESS

WITHIN THE DEPARTMENT OF STATE

CHRIS ARGYRIS

DEPARTMENT OF STATE ● WASHINGTON

Contents

Preface

Few of us have the objectivity to stand back sufficiently far from the organizations in which we work to see these organizations as living systems of people; people relating to each other, relating to the organizational structure, to the world that impinges upon our daily environment. Even granting ourselves this objectivity—this needed distance and time—for meaningful self-examination, we must be concerned with whether it is possible for us to bring sufficient experience to produce helpful, useful information.

The Department of State has been fortunate to have had Dr. Chris Argyris of Yale step out of the academic ranks, even if briefly, to devote his wide background in the behavioral sciences and in administrative practices, to serve us as a kind of alter ego. And I mean an alter ego in the finest sense of that phrase: as a friend and confidant.

The efforts in organizational development, and the examination of the Foreign Service which engaged Chris Argyris' attention stem from an exploratory kind of seminar held at Airlie House in mid-summer of 1964. At that meeting some 20 senior Foreign Service Officers began to explore some of the means by which they, as individuals, using ideas developed in the social and behavioral sciences, could relate to their work, their co-workers, and their organization in new and significant ways.

Since then several hundred officers of the Department of State have taken part in such training experiences. I have done so myself, and I think, along with me, that most of these officers would subscribe to the thesis that, although one may have little doubt concerning one's professional capability when each day's crises arise, it is only slightly short of a revelation to search out and perhaps to discover our true personal location within the web of organizational relationships we have—the very concerns which have so engrossed the author of this paper for so long.

Eventually a program began to take shape in the Department which is striving to merge the ongoing, inevitable process of organizational evolution with the vital processes of individual development and understanding. Under the banner of "Action for Organizational Development," the Department is pioneering efforts in this field which have aroused the attention of major segments of the business community and of the Government. Indeed, we now find ourselves in the unusual role of breaking new ground in the creation of what may prove to be one model for organizational change and growth in any large organization.

In this analysis of the "living system" of the Department of State, Dr. Argyris frequently quotes individual points of view expressed by one of the participants in his seminars. The reader will quickly note that many of these are candid, sometimes critical, viewpoints. They exist within a prevailing climate dedicated to positive attitudes toward the organization.

The decision to publish a study of this kind, or to publish it without censoring the quotations, was not taken lightly. Large organizations in general are not noted for being candid about internal problems and differing viewpoints. We also recognized the fact that the sessions in which this material was developed were problem-oriented. This naturally produced a strong bias in favor of what was wrong with the system. As a result many of the good things about the system including its strengths and the deep dedication of its people or the prevalence of positive attitudes about the organization are not reflected in the paper. It would have been much easier not to publish Dr. Argyris' work out of fear that the material might be twisted out of context or otherwise treated unsympathetically.

Several factors mitigated against such a conservative response.

The first was the realization that, if we really are breaking new ground in our organizational development program, it would behoove us to take this risk, to be open about the ambivalent attitudes, feelings, and frustrations of the people who constitute the living system.

A second realization was that the quotations appearing in this work, with minor changes of time and place, could have been uttered by persons in any large organization; that what we are dealing with here are problems typical of all large enterprises (private and public) and not alone of the Department of State. This, indeed, is a point that Dr. Argyris himself stresses.

Finally, the most positive reason is that being honest and open about the problems dealt with in this study offers the best beginning for dealing with them effectively and constructively. Students of organizations have long been aware that the "informal" life of attitudes and relationships is just as important in large organizations, if not more important, than the formal life of structure and procedure. The real sin is to pretend that the informal life—or the living system, if you prefer—either does not exist or does not require the attention of management.

One cannot capture a river in a bucket although a bucket can provide a partial sample of what is in a river. These are one skilled observer's views of a highly complex, diversified organization; an expert observer's partial sample. They are presented in the hope that they will be tested against the Department's collective experience to stimulate a continuing examination which will improve this essential institution through which we all serve the American people.

We shall need the understanding and support of all its members if we are to achieve the goals we mutually seek.

William J. Crockett
Deputy Under Secretary for Administration

A Note to the Reader*

During 1965 three Airlie House management conferences were held. Each was attended by 20 senior Foreign Service officers. (About 75 percent were Foreign Service officers of Class I and Career Ministers. The remainder were Foreign Service officers, Class II). The purpose of the conferences was to help the participants enhance their competence in dealing with people and managing systems (such as embassies, regional bureaus, functional departments).

The participants spent many hours in looking at their own behavior, in examining carefully their styles of leading people, and in exploring the causes of organizational effectiveness and ineffectiveness within the State Department. As many of the participants have already attested directly to the Deputy Under Secretary of State, they had never been in such an intense, personal self, and organizational examination in all their lives.

During the discussions, the men diagnosed with earnestness and commitment their personal limitations as leaders of people, as well as the problems of the State Department as an organization. The richness of the problems diagnosed and insights developed defies description in a short report. Many of the participants wondered if some organized summary of the conferences could not be produced. Since the sessions were taped, I promised to listen to them, take detailed notes, and attempt to write a report. The work that follows is an attempt to bring together some of the major findings as I interpreted them. In order to minimize the inherent limitations in reporting and analyzing such a complex experience, I followed several simple rules. I remained as close as I could to data that was on tape and to which I could refer for illustrations. Only those problems that were validated by the majority of the members have been included. The quotations that describe the problem are taken from several sessions so that they do not represent the

---

*This report was to become the basis for a more thorough and systematic study. However, I was asked by my University to take on certain assignments that forced the cancellation of the year planned for research.

views of only one group. Needless to say, I alone should be held responsible for the limitations of this report, since it is my view and analysis of the proceedings.

The skeptical reader might wonder if the data are not distorted because the Foreign Service officers tried to give us those data which they thought would fit within the biases of the faculty. Such a view seriously overlooks the initial resistance of the majority of the officers who openly questioned the value of discussing management problems. For them, the substantive issues were the important ones.

Also it overlooks the fact that many of these men became intensely involved in becoming more aware of themselves as people and as leaders. The depth to which some went into this process can be illustrated by the comment of one man who said, "I learned that it is one thing to mistrust people when one is capable of trusting, and quite another to mistrust when one is not capable of trusting. I was in the latter group."

The more comfortable the men became in this new area of examining their behavior and their organization, the higher became their standards of what they would accept as valid. Nothing was left unchallenged. Actual examples were constantly requested. The behavior of the participants was freely called into play as evidence for or against a point. Thus one group listened to the tape of a session in which one of their members became angry and hostile to most of them. They found that they withdrew from him and became more passive. In another case they tried to evaluate each other's behavior but found it extremely difficult, especially when they felt this might embarrass the other. These two examples provided the group with living confirmation that (1) they did tend to withdraw from hostility, and (2) they were uncomfortable coping with feelings.

In addition to providing a summary of some of the discussions at the conferences, I hope that the report will provide the basis for the development of further action recommendations from within the Foreign Service. In Section 4 I have made eight recommendations, but primarily I have focused upon the problem areas. Focusing on the ineffective and negative runs the risk that some reader (especially a non-alumnus of the conferences) may interpret the analysis as pessimistic and hopeless. Nothing could be further from the truth. Although it is true that I present a diagnosis of a human social system that seems self-maintaining and somewhat closed, I am very optimistic about action steps that can be taken (and some already have been taken) to bring about effective change.

Nor do I mean to leave the impression of being condemning, especially of the Foreign Service Corps. I have come to respect deeply the professional competence, personal commitment, and constructive intent of the overwhelming number of Foreign Service personnel with whom I interacted. Indeed, I believe that a major source of strength for the State Department is the Foreign Service Corps. The best evidence for this is in the deep and incisive analysis that the participants helped to develop about their organization.

Finally, the diagnosis developed from the tapes was supported by the reports of 31 junior Foreign Service officers who had no contact with their senior counterparts on matters affecting this study. Another type of corroboration is the fact that many of the problems that are described herein have been found in many of the largest corporations in our country. Thus the State Department is by no means alone or unique in the problems described below.

Because the Foreign Service Corps has been the target for unfair criticisms by outsiders, I feel compelled to make it explicit that this analysis focuses on the State Department as a social system and not upon the Foreign Service officers as individuals. Although, as the reader will see, I will be somewhat critical of parts of the Foreign Service as a system, I want to clearly disassociate myself from the critics of the State Department who believe that the Foreign Service cannot change itself. As a result of my work with the Foreign Service officers I have come to respect their intellectual integrity, their strength of character, exemplified by their willingness to dig deeply into their own organization in order to set the foundations for its future development.

I hope that this report helps to bring about those internal organizational changes that will build upon, maximize the creativity of, and reward the dedication with which the Foreign Service personnel work. I would also like to take this occasion to thank all the people who helped me to learn so much about the State Department.

1

Introduction

Secretary Rusk has told his Business Advisory Council that one of his biggest problems is getting people to accept and enlarge their responsibility. Recent analysts have characterized the State Department as being administratively so sluggish that it makes "corridor diplomacy" almost inevitable. Foreign Service officers have spoken to the writer of their fear of being engulfed by "the system" and simultaneously their feelings of hopelessness regarding changes in its makeup. They condemned, for example, "layering," yet they admittedly continued to practice and in some cases expand it. They questioned the selection and promotion processes, yet when asked to provide a viable alternative, they were unable to do so.

Why does the State Department have such difficulties at the moment when it is being asked to enlarge its managerial responsibilities? Historically, the answers have been diagnosed to be poor organizational structure, ineffective personnel and educational policies. The Herter Study, to cite a most recent and respected example, makes specific proposals for changes in the State Department's organizational structure, the staffing of the Foreign Service Corps, and the education of its members. All these are important suggestions. In my opinion, however, they are destined, at best, to have mediocre success; at worst, failure. If anything, they will probably succeed in increasing the Foreign Service community's fear of another reorganization, their uncertainty of its usefulness, and their feelings of helplessness in preventing it from occurring again. The difficulty does not lie in the recommendations; all of them are relevant and important. The difficulty resides in the fact

1

that the organization will not be able to integrate these recommendations effectively unless the interpersonal milieu is altered.

Why do I make such a gloomy prediction? Because the living system of the State Department in general, and of the Foreign Service in particular, is so constructed that it predisposes the State Department to managerial ineffectiveness. It contains norms that inhibit open confrontation of difficult issues and penalize people who take risks. I intend to show that the living system rewards certain types of interpersonal styles, helps to create a perception of the Foreign Service as being a rather closed club, induces a degree of blindness on the part of the members concerning their impact on each other and "outsiders," and generates an intricate network of organizational defenses that makes the members believe that changing it may be very difficult if not impossible.

What is the living system of an organization? Briefly, it is the way people actually behave, the way they actually think and feel, the way they actually deal with each other. It includes both the formal and the informal activities. The living system represents how things are, not merely how they are supposed to be. It includes all the relevant behavior that can be observed as people administer each other's efforts in order to achieve the goals of the organization.*

---

*As the Airlie House alumni may recall, I presented a view that the way modern organizations are designed, built, and administered, inevitably creates forces toward ineffectiveness and organizational illness. I am not using that argument in this paper because it would be repetitive. I believe that the problems described in this report compound the felony committed by the traditional organizational structure and managerial controls used by the State Department. (Chris Argyris, Integrating the Individual and the Organization (John Wiley and Sons, 1964).

2

I.

The Norms of the Living System
of the Foreign Service

Every living system has a set of norms created and maintained by the members. The norms act to make behavior understandable to, and manageable by, the members of the system. Norms may be likened to streets in a community. Once a street is created it acts to coerce people to drive on it rather than on the sidewalk.

Although norms tend to be experienced by the members as coercive, understanding them does not mean that we can explain all the possible behavior. Individuals differ in the clarity with which they see the norms, in the degree to which they will abide by them, and the feelings they will experience in following or violating them. All one can say when one has identified the norms is that he has increased his probability of explanation somewhat beyond chance. The exact degree of prediction possible depends on how accurately one has ascertained the norms and the degree to which the participants have their behavior guided by the norms.

Norms are especially helpful in predicting behavior of individuals under conditions of individual or system stress. Under stress people tend to look for support just as more of the formal law tends to become part of the living law when crime increases. In an organization decisions that require individuals to take risks, to enlarge their responsibility, to decide under highly ambiguous or frequently changing conditions all produce conditions of stress. To someone who wants to understand the effectiveness of a system, these stressful conditions are very important.

The norms described below were included only when the majority of the individuals agreed that they existed. The criterion for existence was that they had seen people's behavior guided by the norms. This behavior did not necessarily have to be their own, although as one can see from the comments below, many of the participants owned up to being influenced by the norms.

WITHDRAWAL FROM INTERPERSONAL DIFFICULTIES AND CONFLICT

The first norm cited was the tendency to withdraw from open discussion of interpersonal difficulties and conflict. This withdrawal eventually included <u>substantive</u> issues that might, if discussed forthrightly, create conflict or interpersonal embarrassment.

As can be seen from the excerpts below, the withdrawal from direct confrontation of issues can lead to all types of bureaucratic maneuverings to reach people "indirectly," "carefully," "safely." For example:

A. If I sense that I am not getting through, if the other person has his hearing aid shut off, I find myself feeling irritated. Then, I quickly sober down and begin to calculate how I can get through. I find out his weaknesses by talking with others. I may seek a third party who might be held in higher esteem and who might get my message across to him. I may hold off until I can have a particular meeting held in which he has to listen . . .

B. Let me cut you off and add when I use that I usually see to it that the right people are invited so that the weight of unanimity of opinion hits him . . .

C. Yes, but I've been on the receiving end of such meetings and could sense they were loaded so I mistrusted what was going on. I therefore asked more time to study the issue.

D. Come on, now, do all of you mean to say that you wouldn't confront the man directly?

E. Well, if he is a very close friend, I wouldn't mind . . .

B. Like hell! Let's admit it—we rarely even confront our very close friends if we think they're turning us off.

MINIMUM INTERPERSONAL OPENNESS, LEVELING, AND TRUST

The second norm may be characterized as <u>not</u> being open about <u>interpersonal problems or substantive issues that can be threatening to people, especially superiors and peers.</u> The low degree of openness over long periods of time can make it difficult for people to know how much faith to place in what others are saying. This, in turn, can lead to few people wishing to take risks, to experiment. With a low degree of risk-taking and experimenting, trust will also be low.

A. If I were to be very honest, I think that one reason I have succeeded is that I have learned <u>not</u> to be open; <u>not</u> to be candid. Do the powers that be realize what you fellows (turning to the staff) are implying—that we should strive to be more open? That's like asking us to commit organizational suicide.

B. I agree with A. I have experienced situations where I sensed the superior was not leveling. I figured that he was trying to set up either a psychological situation which would predispose me to his point of view, or he was trying to set up a situation where only one conclusion was possible.

C. And what did you say?

B. Not a darn thing—I let him continue.

D. The superior may be doing it unconsciously.

B. In the situations that I recall, it was conscious.

D. How did you know?

B. He was flustered.

F. Another problem is that many of us have been taught never to level so that we can negotiate. I frequently feel that the man is not leveling, not because he lacks ideas but because he is negotiating. He is not presenting all the relevant factors because he is intent on achieving certain results.

5

C.   And, again let me ask you, do you question him about your inferences?

F.   Of course not. I let him go on thinking he is succeeding.

D.   Maybe he knows that you know that he is not leveling.

A.   Then we're in a silly bind. He might as well be open.

In one group an incident occurred which led one ambassador to ask if, after living in such a system for many years, it might not be difficult for someone to be open with his superior because he would run the risk of being accused by the superior of not having been open previously.

A.   Over the years, I developed a lot of evidence that my superior wasn't really leveling. It got so bad that one day I seriously thought of resigning. But I didn't have the courage. I didn't ever tell him this.

B.   Why not?

A.   It would upset him.

B.   How would you feel about telling him?

A.   I suppose it would not be easy for me—but I could do it.

B.   But won't you also have the problem that when you finally leveled with him, you, too, had not been open up to that point? He could argue that when you were under stress you did to him exactly what you resent he does to you.

A.   (becomes red) I never thought of that.

MISTRUST OF OTHERS' AGGRESSIVENESS AND FIGHTING

The third characteristic that dominated the living system was that the appropriate reaction to aggressive fighting or openly competitive behavior was to distrust it and to withdraw from active confrontation.

For example, if someone becomes angry during a meeting, the appropriate behavior is either to pardon him openly (and covertly condemn him); or to see his aggressiveness as an act, a ploy, a conscious role-playing to frighten the others.

Unfortunately, such a response tends to make the man who became angry even angrier. This may cause further withdrawal and disbelief, by the majority, of the validity of the individual's aggressiveness. This, in turn, frustrates even more the man who in the first place became hostile.

How is he to react? He knows that in becoming angry he is running the risk of negative evaluation by others. One strategy is to hold back his feelings. However, if he does lose control and his feelings come out, he runs the risk of being negatively evaluated by others because he could not control his behavior. If the others react by (1) "pardoning his feelings," (2) disbelieving his behavior, and (3) assuming that it is an act, the aggressor will probably become even more furious and more hostile. The majority then can rightly feel incensed and even more justified in their negative evaluations. ("We are trying to help this person by being polite and remaining objective, and all he does is criticize us.")

As these ways of reacting became evident, the men reported that they soon learned to mistrust their own and others' politeness, manifested under stress. After all, if their own politeness was a facade, then maybe this was true of the others. This mistrust acted to deepen the feelings of distance between people and increase ambiguity in interpersonal relations.

A. I tend to distrust people who enjoy selling and fighting. I can remember several cases which we lost because they were using these tactics. We resented it.

B. What did you do?

A. Nothing. What can you say—you resent competing and fighting? You know their answer would be, "Well, that's the trouble with you State Department types."

C. This is an interesting issue. ——'s basic technique is to needle and challenge us so that we can respond. How do we feel about it? Personally, if I may be blunt, I don't like it. I think he is showing a weakness.

D. How can he show strength?

C. By remaining cool, calm, and objective.

E. (an aggressive, competitive person) I know some of you don't like my style but I would like to hear your views. Frankly, I've been part of failures and successes. In all the successes we won because we were willing to get volatile and fight.

C. I would imagine in State we'd say that you lost if you became volatile and emotional.

WITHDRAWAL FROM AGGRESSIVENESS AND FIGHTING

As one might expect from the discussion above, a norm also exists suggesting that the appropriate response to aggressiveness is to withdraw and to judge the individual negatively but not to tell him.   One can imagine the impact of such a response when and if the man who has done the withdrawing is some day in the position of filling out a performance evaluation.

A. I'm one of these fellows that go at things hammer and tongs. I tell you, there's nothing more upsetting than suddenly realizing that the guys I have badgered have no response—just silence.

B. So for you, our silence hurts.

A. It hurts deep.

Mr. A fought openly to develop a position and get agreement.   In the process he became emotional, aggressive, and sometimes hostile.   The more he continued, the more people withdrew.   The faculty member pointed this out and asked if there were any other way to deal with A's style.

B. Well, the only way I dealt with him was to say to myself, "If you're so emotional about this, so sure of yourself, —heavens! You'll never listen to me."

C. I resented his "selling."

D. I withdrew.

E. So did I.

F. What's all this about withdrawing? I haven't had any sense of withdrawal.

A. Well, I have felt that people withdrew. Right now most of this group does not seem involved. If the (faculty

8

member) had not brought it up, I doubt if this issue of withdrawal would have been discussed.

D. In my opinion, whether I withdraw or not depends on the situation.   When I see someone get as emotional and persuasive as you do, I tend to withdraw.

A. Which, as I said before, only irritates me even more.

B. This is interesting.   I'd like to raise a further point. I think all of us have disagreed with the way —— works. I have a sneaking suspicion we each sat back and said, "I deal with my subordinates satisfactorily and to hell with ——."   In my case I even said I wouldn't want to be ——'s subordinate.   Now I would never have said this before.

A. But I sensed that you wouldn't.   I felt it.

D. My reaction to you—now that we are leveling—was, "Goodness, is this the way the guy really thinks and operates?"   My second reaction was to tell myself to relax and let the conversation continue.

A. But you weren't going to level.

D. No, because I believe that constructive discussion cannot arise out of conflict.

II.

The Values of the Foreign Service About

Effective Human Relationships

All human beings hold certain values about what are and are not effective human relationships. These values are internalized commands which tend to have a strong coercive effect on the way individuals choose to behave. Values are usually learned in early life. The inter-relationship between values and system norms tends to be very high because individuals tend to choose consciously (and unconsciously) those professions and those systems whose norms are congruent with their values.

To put this another way, the values described below were held by the Foreign Service officer long before he entered the Foreign Service; indeed he probably entered the Service partially because its norms and their values tended to be highly consonant.

THE SUBSTANTIVE SIDE OF THE ORGANIZATION
IS PARAMOUNT

The most important behavior is related to the substantive activity of the Foreign Service. The management of people and physical resources, the building of a viable management system, are second-class activities. Typical examples:

Important as management may be, it should never be our objective; management, at best, is a tool of substance and should always be subservient to substance.

Some of us are concerned that management is becoming a major objective in the Foreign Service. I think most of us in the profession feel that our objective is conducting relationships with foreign countries.

Each one of us, if I may say so, is a manager. We never think of ourselves—no, that's wrong—we rarely think of ourselves as managers. Not only do we not think of ourselves as managers, but we are willing to accept the fact that other people say we aren't. And so when somebody says there are only two good executives in the entire Foreign Service, we accept it. I heard this statement made and none of us questioned it.

TO BE RATIONAL IS TO BE EFFECTIVE; TO BE EMOTIONAL IS TO BE INEFFECTIVE

The second norm emphasized by the respondents is that human beings are most effective when they are rational. They are least effective when they become emotional or permit others to do so. Interpersonal relationships and "personalities" should be kept out of everyday relationships. Typical comments:

I must confess to one type of inhibition that I do feel keenly. I do feel inhibited in talking and dealing with personal relationships that involve people's feelings.

People should keep personalities out of their work.

Mature people are people who can control their feelings and not let them get in the way of rational discussion and reason.

In another context:

When Foreign Service personnel were asked:	The majority responded— variously:
1. When disagreement erupts into personal antagonisms, what is the best thing for a leader to do ?	1. "Get them back to the facts." "Keep personalities out of the discussion." "Call off the meeting."

2. How they would deal with a
   briefing officer who goes into
   irrelevancies.

2. "I would carefully stop him."
   or "I would diplomatically
   change the subject."

3. If two responsible officers
   were polarized on an issue
   and felt very strongly about it,
   what should their superior do?

3. "I would have a cooling-off
   period." "See if I could deal
   with each through a third party
   to arbitrate and make a
   decision."

4. If a superior held a position
   with which the subordinate did
   not agree, what should the
   subordinate do?

4. "Be careful about openly dis-
   agreeing." "Don't make
   waves."

The preferred response is one that suppresses emotion-
laden issues and interpersonal problems. People should not
discuss the feelings they may be experiencing about each other
while discussing difficult issues. Also, people should try not
to behave in ways that may be upsetting to others. If someone
violates this norm repeatedly, he may be cautioned in a "diplomatic" manner. If his behavior is not changed (and very
little interpersonal behavior can be changed by careful, rational
dialog), then an appropriate note of the man's ineffectiveness
may be placed in his personnel record.

EFFECTIVE LEADERS DIRECT, OVERSEE, CONTROL THE EFFORTS OF THEIR SUBORDINATES

Data to illustrate the third norm was more difficult to obtain.
Typically, when Foreign Service personnel were asked about
effective leadership, they responded with all the correct phrases
such as "the respect for individuals," "the importance of
people," "confidence in people," "helping people take on more
responsibility," "treating people as individuals," etc.
However, when we examined carefully the examples the
respondents gave to illustrate their leadership style, it became apparent that they dominated and controlled people much
more than they helped people to grow and take responsibility.
The domination and control, however, were diplomatic and
polite. The overwhelming majority of the men were unaware
of the gap between their views of their leadership styles and
their actual behavior.

Other illustrations came from the following replies:

When Foreign Service personnel were asked to describe:	The majority responded:
1. An effective leader during a problem-solving meeting.	1. One who controls the meeting, keeps it on the track, controls the pace, etc.
2. One of the primary tasks of the leader.	2. To define clearly for the subordinate his goals, objectives, and scope of responsibility.
3. Subordinate's needs.	3. Strong leadership.

It may interest the reader to know that these same values tend to be held by and with the same lack of awareness by top-level business executives,* physical scientists, engineers, professors, architects, religious leaders, and graduate students.** Thus these values seem to be characteristic of professional people in general and are not peculiar to the Foreign Service.

---

*Chris Argyris, "Interpersonal Barriers to Decision-Making," Harvard Business Review, March-April 1966, pp. 84-98.

**Organization and Innovation, Irwin and Company, 1965.

The Consequences of the Norms and Values

In this section I should like to indicate how the norms of the Foreign Service officers interact to create certain characteristics within the living system of the State Department that can have significant effects upon the effectiveness of Foreign Service activities, substantive and administrative.

I.

Interpersonal Styles to Confront Conflict or Threatening Issues

Partially in order to make their own world more coherent and manageable and partially in order to adapt effectively to whatever living system in which they work, individuals tend to develop certain interpersonal styles. These styles represent preferences that people hold as to how they should behave.

One way to examine interpersonal styles is to describe two ideal types of behavior (not individuals) whose components are on opposite ends of the continua. These ideal types are analytical categories that have been found useful in studying executives and professional people. They do not purport to represent how any particular individual will tend to behave. Clearly no individual should be pigeonholed either as a type A or type B. Moreover, no suggestion is being made that one style is better than the other. Indeed, if one had to take a position, it would be that each type of behavior is effective for certain conditions. Also, an effective Foreign Service officer is probably one who is able to behave effectively in both styles or a combination of styles.

Type A Behavior	Type B Behavior
1. Retreating from his own and others' aggressiveness or hostility.	1. Being aggressive with self and others. Competing with others.
2. Refraining from open expression of positive or negative feelings.	2. Refraining from open expression of positive feelings but willingly expressing negative feelings.
3. Refraining from encouraging others to tell him about his personal impact on them.	3. Refraining from asking for information about own impact, but giving such information to others if asked.
4. Emphasizing primarily the substantive, not the administrative, activities.	4. Emphasizing both substantive and administrative activities.
5. Accepting dependence upon others, especially under conditions of risk-taking.	5. Resisting strongly being dependent on others.
6. Expressing loyalty by being sensitive to the limits and desires of others. A loyal member should not openly hurt others even in the interests of the organization.	6. Expressing loyalty by being committed to organizational goals. A loyal member can openly hurt others in the interests of the organization.

A useful way to use these categories is to ask ourselves, in a world whose norms included withdrawal from interpersonal difficulties and conflict, minimum interpersonal openness and trust, mistrust of others' and own aggressiveness, what kind of behavior would tend to be rewarded within the system? Are there any hypotheses that we can develop as to whether type A or type B behavior will tend to be preferred?

Most of the respondents reported that behavior approximating the characteristics of type A was more adaptive and effective within the Foreign Service's living system. This does not mean that all the respondents constantly behaved in terms of the dimensions represented by type A. Indeed, there was much evidence of individual differences. Also reported were several important conditions under which behavior tended to vary. For example, the respondents suggested that the younger the individual, the further away from Washington, the smaller the embassy (up to a certain point), and then the more informal the embassy, the less the tendency to view type A behavior as competent behavior.

Another important moderating factor may be that the Foreign Service officer has learned, from bitter experience, that he cannot depend upon a consistent or clear policy from the highest levels from which to make a decision. Or, he may learn that once having made a decision consonant with the policy he may be reversed for reasons that are not related to foreign policy, and that the reversal may originate outside of the State Department. Such conditions tend to make his world unpredictable and full of ambiguity. Moreover, he may understandably feel concerned about the fact that his superiors do not seem to have adequate influence with people at the upper levels of decision making. One way to deal with conflict and threat in such a world is to select type A behavioral responses, because they decrease the probability of his being unfairly punished and hurt. All these moderating factors need to be studied thoroughly so that their influence can be systematically ascertained.

At the moment, the only systematic data available are the comments of the faculty of the conferences and the quantitative analyses of the tapes. The faculty selected for the Airlie House conferences (and since then for the Tidewater Inn conferences) have been of the highest quality. They have worked with hundreds of groups from all walks of life and at all levels of organizational and social hierarchies. These faculty members are unanimous, so far, that the State Department conferences are the most difficult to unfreeze, i.e., to help the participants to learn to be more open, to take risks, and to help others to do the same. They cite as reasons for this difficulty the participants' relatively strong discomfort in talking about interpersonal issues and feelings, in confronting problems openly, in being aware of themselves, in their willingness to be dependent upon the faculty, and in their strong tendency to intellectualize.

If we compare the quantitative results of the analyses made of the tapes taken from 3 State Department conferences with similar tape analyses from 50 other conferences, we find that the State Department conferences were, indeed, the most difficult to unfreeze. However, once unfrozen the members of the best ones tended to move very fast in becoming more open, expressing feelings, and taking risks. For example, in the graphs below, A represents a typical industrial top executive group that has learned an above average amount

during the conference.   Graph B represents the learning curve
of the best State Department group scored to date.

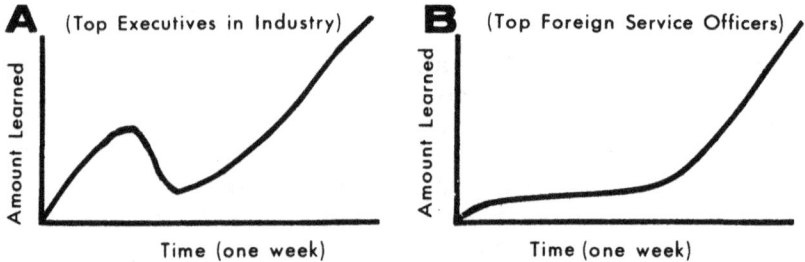

Many of the Foreign Service officers believed that type A
behavior was more effective in diplomatic relationships. Indeed,
many wondered, if one could show a preponderance of type A
behavior, whether it was not due to the fact that such behavior
was required in diplomacy.   This is an interesting point and
merits systematic research.   To my knowledge there exists
no objective description of how the Foreign Service personnel
actually do behave when in a dialog of diplomacy. Nor are there
any studies suggesting that the behavior that may be effective
with representatives of foreign countries is the most effective
in the management of American Foreign Service personnel.
There are two reasons why I question the belief that type
A behavior is the only type that necessarily tends to belong
with effective diplomatic activity.   First, in the small groups
there were some ambassadors who preferred behavior that tended
toward the type B ends of the continua. These men were considered to be very effective by their peers and their superiors.
Thus type B behavior may be functional to diplomacy. Second,
if one analyzes the interesting monograph full of illustrations
by mission chiefs of what worked for them to solve important
problems, one will find some illustrations of type B behavior,
although the strategy most frequently recommended under stress
or in ambiguous situations was type A.*   If I would make a
prediction, it would be that each type of behavior is effective
under certain conditions and these conditions do not necessarily split themselves into administrative and substantive
activities.   One individual, for example, gave an example that
if people within an embassy (of which he was a member) had
leveled with each other and the embassy with Washington, a

---

*"This Worked for Me. . .," U.S. Department of State (introduction by
William J. Crockett), Washington, D.C., 1964.

trip made by a President of the United States would probably not have been made.

One final point about styles of interpersonal relationships. Since the administrative process tends to be viewed as a second-class process, those in administration tend to feel like second-rate citizens. My observations (which require much systematic research) are that the administrative side tends to be composed of many people who indeed are doing second-class (and in some cases second-rate) work. These people and these jobs tend to be at the lower levels. At the upper levels of the administrative hierarchy there are many dedicated, highly competent, intensely professional individuals. They are committed to making the State Department a more flexible, viable system. However, they feel frustrated, and at times hurt and rejected, because of the second-rate status accorded to them and their function by the majority of the Foreign Service personnel. Under these conditions, it may be that a more B type of interpersonal style is necessary to survive and to get the work done. Thus it may be that, if an empirical study were made, one would find in the top administrative area more behavior approximating the B ends of the continua.*

An interesting example of the difficulties that exist between the substantive and the administrative "sides" was obtained from a recent State Department conference similar to the Airlie House conferences. The group was divided into two subgroups. Group A was composed primarily of top-level substantive officers. Group B was composed primarily of top-level administrative officers. Each group was asked to discuss three questions and to develop a list of words or phrases that would summarize their answers. These lists were then to be shared with the other group. The three questions were:

1.   What qualities best describe our group?

2.   What qualities best describe the other group?

3.   What qualities do we predict the other group would assign to us?

The faculty reported that the groups became involved in the exercise and produced products that reflected validly the discussions that were held in their separate meeting rooms.

---

*It may also be interesting to note that all the political appointees tended to prefer an interpersonal style that approximated more of B than A.

The results were as follows:

The substantive officers saw themselves as:

1. Reflective
2. Qualitative
3. Humanistic—subjective
4. Cultural—broad interests
5. Generalizers
6. Intercultural sensitivity
7. Detached from personal conflicts

The substantive officers saw the administrative officers as:

1. Doers and implementers
2. Quantitative
3. Decisive and forceful
4. Non-cultural
5. Limited goals
6. Jealous of us
7. Interested in form more than substance
8. Wave of the future! (exclamation mark theirs)
9. Drones but necessary evils

The substantive officers predicted that the administrative officers would see them as:

1. Arrogant—snobs
2. Intellectuals
3. Cliquish
4. Resistant to change
5. Inefficient—dysfunctional
6. Vacillating and compromising
7. Effete

The administrative officers saw themselves as:

1. Decisive—guts
2. Resourceful—adaptive
3. Pragmatic
4. Service-oriented
5. Ability to get along
6. Receptiveness to change
7. Dedicated to job
8. Misunderstood
9. Useful
10. Modest! (added by the individual doing the presenting)

The administrative officers saw the substantive officers as:

1. Masked—isolated
2. Resourceful—serious
3. Respected
4. Inclination to stability
5. Dedication to job
6. Necessary
7. Externally oriented
8. Cautious
9. Rational
10. Surrounded by mystique
11. Manipulative
12. Defensive

The administrative officers predicted that the substantive officers would see them as:

1. Necessary evil
2. Defensive—inflexible
3. Preoccupied with minutiae
4. Negative and bureaucratic
5. Limited perspective
6. Less cultural (educated clerks)
7. Misunderstood
8. Practical
9. Protected
10. Resourceful

II.

Success and Failure in the Living System

If we examine the norms and the interpersonal styles we see that there is a remarkably close fit between the former and interpersonal style A. From other behavioral science research we can predict in general that those who prefer type A interpersonal style will tend to feel that they are valued, rewarded, and protected by the system. They will tend to feel that some of the deepest aspects of their selves are confirmed by the system. They will also tend to feel interpersonally competent in the system.

The feelings of being interpersonally competent, valued, rewarded, and confirmed will tend to lead those who prefer type A behavior to feel a high degree of (a) personal effectiveness in dealing with people, (b) commitment to the living system of the Foreign Service, and (c) cohesiveness with other type A's in the Foreign Service. Recalling our previous statement that the majority of the respondents preferred interpersonal style A, then we may conclude that the majority of the respondents probably were highly involved with, and felt very closely identified with, the living system of the Foreign Service.

Turning to the minority who preferred interpersonal style B, the opposite is true. They do not tend to feel that their preferred style is valued, rewarded, protected, or confirmed. They do not tend to feel, interpersonally speaking, very competent. Understandably, they report that they feel little effectiveness in dealing with many Foreign Service officers, as well as little commitment and cohesiveness with the living system. Many feel alien to the norms of the system.

Most type B's are aware that they cannot adapt with open hostility toward the norms and the system. This could mean professional suicide, since most of the rewards and promotions are controlled by Foreign Service personnel who prefer type A behavior. Consequently, most adapt (1) by seeking to join those departments where there are many others who prefer type B*, (2) by developing contacts outside the Foreign Service Corps but within the State Department, or in agencies outside the State Department, where they can freely be critical of the norms of their system, and (3) by striving to change the administrative and personnel policies and practices that, to date, favor the existing norms.

But none of these adaptive activities is adequate. Most of their everyday dealings are with members of the Foreign Service. They cannot run away from them. Moreover, striving to change policies and practices could place them in a negative light in the eyes of the majority of the Foreign Service personnel. This, in turn, causes them to be seen by the majority of the Foreign Service as unpredictable, somewhat unstable, and perhaps a little immature. The B's sense these evaluations and dislike them for two reasons. One, they do not feel they will succeed if they are perceived in this negative light. Two, if they face reality, they will have to admit that they <u>are</u> behaving in unstable, unpredictable ways and that under stress they <u>are</u> unable to control their behavior. They realize that this violates the norms of effective behavior within the system, as well as their view of effective action.

But even if crises are not frequent, this adaptive strategy can create problems at a deeper level because many may feel that they have conformed to cultural norms and pressures from others, in which they do not believe and which they do not value. They cannot escape the fact that they are behaving non-genuinely in order to survive or get ahead. This admission would be especially repugnant to type B's who dislike being dependent. Soon they may come to dislike the A's and themselves. Under these conditions they may become supersensitive about the Foreign Service Corps, and see it as an unwieldly, rigid, unchangeable, ineffective system. This may act to reinforce their need to change it; to rid the service of the dominance

---

*Foreign Service Officers tended to agree, during meetings held to discuss this report, that departments and bureaus differed in terms of the degree to which they attracted and kept individuals with strong preference toward styles A or B. It was interesting to note, however, that no agreement was reached as to which bureau preferred A's and which preferred "type B's" while the other groups preferred "type A's."

of the present norms; to make a service which also rewards their interpersonal style.

The majority of the Foreign Service employees, who value the present norms, react negatively to these activities. Indeed, they may come to view the behavior above as immature, irrational, competitive, ineffective, childish, and disloyal. They may even begin to feel strongly that the Foreign Service should not admit people with such behavior into its ranks, or at least, not reward it. This, in turn, will cause the majority to have stronger "in" feelings; to see their system as healthy and effective; to see the B's as deviants. Once this behavior is identified as deviant, the majority will have developed rational reasons for the necessity of protecting the system from the minority. The minority, in turn, will tend to see the majority reaction as proof that the system is defensive and rigid. Thus we have two subsystems, whose members reinforce organizational divisiveness by self-fulfilling prophecies.

The pressure to protect the system can easily become so strong that the type A's unpremeditatedly (and probably unconsciously) look for, seek out, reward and encourage Foreign Service personnel who do not violate the existing norms. Such a reaction can be seen by outsiders as the Foreign Service developing its own inbred club. Since the open discussion of such emotion-laden issues tends to violate the norms of the system, these issues will not be dealt with openly. Unwittingly, both sides have helped to develop a system whose parts will be spending so much time defending themselves that it will appear, to the outsider, that the system is focused on "exploring its navel," and is against change.

III.

Unawareness of Discomfort With Feelings and of One's Personal Impact Upon Others

In a world where feelings tend to be suppressed, where openness and emotionality are guarded, and where controlled emotionality is rewarded, it is not surprising to find that many of the respondents tended to be blind to their own degree of discomfort with feelings and interpersonal issues as well as their impact upon their subordinates. For example, in the excerpts below, the men explored how uncomfortable they were with the expression of feelings:

A. I felt that in a little sense—B felt more of a sense of personal embarrassment in talking about himself. I wonder, did you feel this way, B?

B. No.

C. No?

B. No.

D. How do others feel about A's views?

E. Well, I think all of us are uncomfortable to a degree, but I think you (B) are more uncomfortable than the rest of us . . . .

B. Then I certainly haven't been communicating!

E. Or you have—but not the messages that you wish.

F.   I have the same feeling as A has about you.

A.   I must confess that part of the reason for raising this question is the fear, I guess, that the lesson also applies to me. How can B successfully lead a large group if he causes the kinds of reactions he does here and if he is that unaware of them? How can others relate effectively to him? And if they do not, how can he or I get the best out of our people?

E.   This is a good point because I know I would never confront anyone with feelings that I had about him, especially during a meeting.

D.   How can trust be built up among people?

The issue of blindness was discussed further in the example below, and the impact it had upon the subordinates was brought out quite clearly. We also get a hint of how behavioral withdrawal can lead to people's writing memos that were equally cryptic and, at the same time, were assumed to cope with difficult problems at a safe distance.

A.   You know, the more I really think about this issue, the more I realize how much we don't listen to what others say.

B.   It happens every day to me. I do it and others do it to me. Almost at any meeting. Nobody listens to what others say.

C.   I wonder if, in the process of turning out, we aren't demonstrating some arrogance which is clearly transmitted. For example, my economic officer starts every day from A and works through to Z. I see him coming through the door and I am usually very busy. I turn myself off.

A.   You know, we on overseas duty live in a particularly pleasant situation. As an ambassador at a post you think you have the attention of all those under you, as well as the local people, and you become a bit spoiled.

B.   Yes, and maybe this is a reason why I insist on short memoranda, not oral presentations. In an oral presentation you waste time. It is much easier, much more precise to note something on a little piece of paper sent me.

C. What we are saying is raising questions if it is easier and truly more precise.

E. We may be saying that but I am not ready to accept it. I would much rather use a more civilized form of communication, that is, write it down. Then I can decide where the creative part of his ideas are and get to them. Of course, I might be stealing some fun from the economic officer, but I'll bet everyone would be happier.

B. You certainly would be happier! (everyone laughs)

C. I was going to agree with E that we should tune people out. Yet, yesterday when F tuned me out while I was talking, I was mad as hell. It was on my mind all afternoon and finally, as you all know, I confronted him.

In still another discussion:

A. This whole discussion raises a critical point that is relevant to all of us. I am sure that all of us have been in the position — just described. Intellectually we have absolutely no intention in the world but to give the other man a fair break in the presentation of his position. We do not wish to convey to others any personal imputation of incompetence or unsatisfactory behavior, and yet our attitudes and behavior may convey that, even though we do not wish to convey that message.

B. I agree with you. If I am learning anything in these discussions, it is how blind we all are to what we do to others.

D. Yes, but note—not so blind as to what others do to us.

In the final example the men provided meaningful illustrations of the probable impact their interpersonal blindness may have had upon the effectiveness and commitment of their subordinates.

A. Do you think there is another possibility? Instead of tuning people out, we really try to anticipate what they are going to say next. Instead of tuning them out we are trying to think ahead to find out what the problem is, so that we can summarize the whole thing at the end of the discussion and make a decision.

27

B. I'd like to suggest that the higher up the ladder one goes, the more the tendency may exist for reading people out rather than thinking ahead.

C. And I guess there are perfectly good reasons for it. The pressure on the senior officials is great. He may get impatient with a subordinate. A degree of competence as a result of having arrived at the top may make us somewhat more arrogant.

D. I don't think anyone is questioning the pressure on the superiors. What I think I am learning to question is: one, the impact this has upon the remainder of the organization. Second, why can't we deal with these problems openly.

E. Perhaps our error is not in tuning him off but in not explaining carefully enough to him why we do this.

B. I think that I don't deal with these problems openly because I would rather not face the discomfort of . . .

F. In my case, if I have a guy who blocks the group, after the meeting is over, I tell my DCM to keep that clown out of my meetings.

C. And as a DCM who has had that happen to me, I can tell you I have to create all sorts of—what we have come to call organizational defenses—to fulfill that order.

A. Also, if you throw him out, he may turn out to be the guy you need to brief you on a particular piece of, say, legislation.

D. To return to C's point about climbing up the ladder and having some justifiable arrogance—I'll tell you how I feel. I have never felt that I was as articulate as many others. However, I wonder if more experience gives us the right to tune people out. We learned yesterday from our own examples that many good ideas frequently diverge from past experience, so that no matter how much experience a man has accumulated, there should be a compulsion on us to be sure we are giving a good hearing to others.

E. I agree. To be perfectly candid, I, myself, have been guilty in not having done this in relation to my subordinates. Also I have a feeling that my superiors quite often have not been concerned about this problem.

IV.

Unintended Consequences of Withdrawal: Guilt and Lack of Self-Confidence

During the discussions the men became aware that withdrawal from confrontation may be safe organizationally speaking, but psychologically it could have unintended effects. Individuals with the intellectual integrity of the overwhelming majority of these participants are unable to deny to themselves that they withdraw. They may be able to rationalize this withdrawal as the "mature" or "effective" thing to do. But this rationalization cannot remain as an effective defense, especially if the adversaries continue to pressure through more fighting and aggressiveness. Soon the individuals who withdraw have to face themselves. As the men below state, the result for them was a lowering of their self-trust, self-confidence, and, in some cases, an increasing feeling of personal failure and guilt.

A. This business of withdrawal has impacts that we haven't discussed yet. Take the situation I described yesterday. I was angry. I didn't like what I saw. I felt that the new policy would really harm the Foreign Service. I wanted to fight; I discussed it with my wife; yet I could not bring myself to do this. So I ended up with a feeling of total inadequacy on my part. I not only mistrusted Mr. —— , I mistrusted myself.

B. I know the problem you are talking about. I withheld information recently because of my too strong sense of hierarchy. Now I realize this is a great mistake. Not communicating ends up giving me a sense of personal failure.

C. It has the same effect on me. It lowers my own acceptance of myself.

D. I heard this described crudely by someone. You can ---- on FS officers and they take it diplomatically.

B. During this week many of us have complained about —— (back in Washington). All of us have admitted that we have never leveled with him. We have withdrawn.

Up to now, I felt this was right. Now I realize that I may be running away from my responsibility. As I thought of this, I suddenly wondered what would happen if people reacted to me by withdrawing. So I began to wonder if Mr. —— feels lonely; if he senses the withdrawal. Does he feel that many of us feel that like death and taxes Mr. —— will always be with us. If he feels this withdrawal and hostility, no wonder he manipulates us. What else can he do?

V.

The System May Become All-Powerful, Beyond the Control of Its Members

In a living system dominated by a low interpersonal openness, leveling, trust, confrontation; a high withdrawal, mistrust of aggressive, fighting behavior; and a blindness to the superior's negative impact on his subordinates; it is not too difficult for the system to seem beyond the control of the participants. The members come to feel entrapped and controlled by the system, even though they are not able to express clearly the reasons for these feelings. For example:

A. This system is a jungle. There is nothing more cruel than to bring a man back after 15 or 20 years and throw him in this jungle. We ought to teach him how to fight jungle warfare.

B. In my experience, no one is willing to teach you. Maybe the best way to learn is to be thrown in. You think you've understood the system and suddenly you find you haven't. You try to hit it, change it, yell at it, but it seems to go on, undisturbed and largely untouched.

It is understandable why people soon come to write careful and innocuous memos, "round the sharp corners off the telegrams," "learn not to make waves," "minimize risk-taking," "fear taking responsibility," "play the game," and be careful to never become a bum and always remain a hero. The latter two are illustrated in the following:

A. All this talk on being open and leveling is nice—and I'm for motherhood too. But I can tell you, if you get

31

the reputation of having lost several important battles—
no one wants a loser. The word gets around and you
have been ruled off the promotion lists. Soon you learn.
If you want to get back on, be less open and less candid.

B. I doubt this.

C. Well, I don't. What do you think happened to —— ?

D. I have to agree with A that if you get a reputation for
losing, you're in trouble.

F. Does this mean that it is better not to try to win . . . ?

A. As the old —— proverb says, it is better to say nothing
a thousand times than to say something once and be
wrong.

You know, this reminds me of the feeling that I have had
from time to time that competence in gaming is crucial
to success. Gaming is when I select that information to
get you to arrive at my conclusion. I select the foils
for my purposes . . .

B. (cuts A off) . . . and I know it.

A. Of course you do and is it not part of the game for you
not to say anything?

B. Yes, I listen and try to find out what you are trying
to sell. Once I figure that out, I stop listening and
think of my rebuttal.

D. Isn't this business of gaming familiar to all of us in
the writing of position papers?

E. Yes, and I'll bet we have all done it—and been embar-
rassed when we got caught very badly at it.

B. And heroes if we win!

If one feels so strongly about an issue that he cannot suppress
the differences in views, one safe strategy is to polarize the issue
and thus delay, as long as possible, the day when it has to be
solved (because people are uncomfortable in dealing with emo-
tionally loaded situations). As long as the decision is delayed,
no confrontation will occur. And no decision is made. The

longer this lack of confrontation continues, the less each side will be ready to compromise (after all, the boss has gone along with this delay for so many months), and the more willing both sides will be to allow (indeed induce) the boss to make the decision. This reduces the protagonists' responsibility in several ways. First, they do not have to make the decision. Second, they do not have to learn to work together. Third, the responsibility for when the delay was to be ended was not theirs. They can remain heroes to their respective groups.

The situation is even more difficult when we recall that the norms of the culture tend to coerce superiors to appoint impartial arbitrators, who are presumed to be objective, to solve the difficult issues. Thus the protagonists get their irresponsibility and dependence upon their superior confirmed and rewarded.

We have a powerful circular loop, a process within the Foreign Service culture that tends to reinforce the participants to minimize interpersonal threat by minimizing risk-taking, being open and being forthright, as well as minimizing their feelings of responsibility and their willingness to confront conflict openly. This, in turn, tends to reinforce those who have decided to withdraw, play it safe, not make waves, and to do so both in their behavior and in their writing. Under these conditions people soon learn the survival quotient of "checking with everyone," of developing policies that upset no one, of establishing policies in such a way that the superior takes the responsibility for them.

Also, people soon learn to worry less about acting as line subordinates who can stand on their own two feet. They worry much more about keeping their superior out of trouble to the point that many line subordinates make themselves, in fact, staff assistants to their superiors. This stance reinforces dependence and conformity. It also coerces "layering," because (1) subordinates staff to be ready for a crisis, (2) more people are needed to make a decision, and (3) protection of one's bureaucratic skin becomes critical for survival.

This network of interconnected coercive processes creates a tight system with the ability to make individuals behave according to the system's demands. All participants now will experience the system as all-powerful and unchangeable. Although they may dislike the system, they will tend to feel a sense of helplessness and resignation about changing it.

Under these conditions the promotion process will tend to be mistrusted. The mistrust will tend to exist within the subordinate and the superior. Each will wonder if the other is leveling; if the superior is judging the subordinate accurately, if the superior is evaluating people primarily in ways to defend himself. For example:

A. One of the things I find difficult to trust is efficiency ratings. I know, in making them out, I have been careful. Part of the problem is that I don't know how my comments will be used.

B. On top of this is a new problem made painfully clear this week. So many of our ratings are defenses of our own styles.

C. I can tell you I fear the efficiency rating process. I think back that I've had two superiors who prided themselves as being consultative in their approach.

I guessed that both said something about me that they felt I might not like. Since both talked about participation, I decided to ask them openly to discuss it. One refused and the second gave the report as he walked out of the Embassy. Neither one of them had the guts to sit down with me in a face-to-face confrontation.

D. I don't think efficiency ratings per se are bad. It is the way they are used that destroys trust.

E. Well, we can all agree, but if I were to be forthright I would have to admit I have not handled the efficiency ratings very effectively. One of my problems is that I would have never thought of discussing interpersonal issues. I always found them embarrassing—and I think the other person does also.

F. I'll tell you what I mistrust in the efficiency ratings. I mistrust the man who rates me. He handles it as if he is making a very careful effort to use precisely the right words, so as not to disturb me. This carries with me an implication of a lack of confidence in me. This causes me to resist.

Another consequence of the above is that group meetings come to be less effective. Participants play it safe. The range of ideas before the meeting is by no means reflected in what goes on in the meetings. Also, commitments are made in the meetings which are diplomatically renounced after the meetings. Diplomatic maneuvering is frequent, especially outside of meetings. Indeed, decisions are really made in small meetings outside of the group. The major purpose for the total group meeting is usually to inform people and to pour ''holy water'' over decisions already made.

This misuse of the group reduces the members' confidence in its effectiveness and increases their defensive maneuverings and dependence on their superior. Each member of a department focuses more on protecting his department than on making effective decisions. Men can make reputations as being skillful, articulate, in-fighting Foreign Service officers who know how to present their case so that their group rarely loses a bureaucratic struggle. The criterion for success is now more in terms of bureaucratic politics then the merits of the case. These decision-making difficulties and sluggishness become especially noticeable when different functional groups must work together to solve a particular problem.

3

The Young Foreign Service Officer

In discussing interpersonal styles, many respondents pointed out that the Foreign Service was changing. One sign of the change was that the younger men tended to be different in style (preferred behavior closer to B) as well as in academic preparation. If their hypothesis regarding style is valid, then one would expect the younger men to be especially frustrated and unhappy with the system. In order to obtain some views, I interviewed in groups and individually 31 officers at levels 7 and 8, including 11 who were so new they were undergoing their orientation and induction into the Service.

Since these interviews were held 6 months before the proceeding analysis was contemplated, the questions asked were not derived from it. This limitation has a strength in that the data obtained can be used as a partial validity check of this analysis. The tactic taken during the interview was to permit the interviewee to discuss any areas that he felt were important if someone wanted to understand the Foreign Service from the younger officer's view. Obviously, not all the issues brought up during the laboratories were discussed in these interviews. However, what impressed me was the relatively high agreement on the critical problems. Also, it was encouraging to see that the younger officer developed no views that contradicted the analysis in Sections 1 and 2.

Turning to the results, the young Foreign Service officers confirmed that the living system was characterized by (1) suppression of interpersonal issues, (2) minimal openness and trust, (3) withdrawal from interpersonal difficulties and conflict, (4) minimal risk-taking and accepting responsibility,

(5) dependence upon the superior, (6) crisis-orientation, (7) writing memos cautiously, and (8) "don't make waves."

In order to give the reader an impression of their reactions, I have included below a composite of the more frequently expressed points of view.

SUPPRESSING EMOTIONS AND INTERPERSONAL ISSUES

Open hostility is not very good form. Negative comments are always made subtly. Until I came here I never placed my ideas in such cautious language. Sometimes I think that one of the advantages of working in my area is that the foreign country is not considered friendly to the U.S. and therefore it is more acceptable to be more open and critical.

———

There is an atmosphere of caution. I would never be open with anyone about his impact on people.

I think it may be a good idea not to have open relationships with people. After all, we live and work with each other for nearly 24 hours a day. In the field we live close to each other. If people were open we might have terrible morale problems.

———

Most Foreign Service officers are competent in their area of specialty. They are capable of seeing issues. Many are also strong enough not to be bound up by the historical past of a particular policy. But few want to offend. That is the most difficult barrier to overcome.

———

With the difficult superior you have to learn to adapt. For example, last week I wrote one of my most important documents and I didn't put down everything I believed because I knew it would only be ignored. I discussed the important ideas with my associates to check them out and get them off my chest.

Researcher: Could you talk to your superior to discuss this problem?

Respondent: I wondered about that and I talked to some others and concluded that he would probably listen to me; agree or disagree, or more likely, accept it and when I leave, ignore it.

So far I have not been happy in my first 5 years. I had these hide-bound bosses for 3 out of the 4 years in —— area.

If you cannot get through to your boss because you feel he does not want to listen, the best thing is to talk to your peers—even those who don't have any influence but whose intellectual capacities you respect.

———————

Frustration and hostility must always be sublimated. It is, as one senior man once told me, "very bad form to express." So you go through life with some long-simmering frustrations. I am amazed at how much contempt can exist, yet people get along quite well on the surface.

———————

Senior people are rarely open. So you have to discount what they say.

People may knife you in the back but never face to face.

CONFORMITY, RESISTANCE TO TAKING RISKS AND RESPONSIBILITY

One thing too many of us learn early is that to make real changes you may have to be a wave maker and that's dangerous. It could harm your career. So many of the senior officers seem to spend their life interest on running an embassy like a tight but nice ship.

If someone is incompetent, he is not fired. He is given an assistant who will do most of the work.

———————

Some superiors—I'd say the majority that I know about—send everything upstairs. Even the most trivial things. Superiors send them upstairs for approval for fear of sticking their necks out.

Much depends upon who is your boss. On balance, there is strong pressure to keep your mouth shut because you may be labeled as an unrealistic thinker.

I am told that a new man can express a way-out idea with less danger because no one expects him to be correct.

I have learned to adapt to the superior who lacks imagination and looks at things in hide-bound ways. The only way this is changed is by changing people.

If you make a way-out point, there are three possible reactions.

1. Most likely it will be listened to; accepted in varying degrees; but you will not be clear about the degree of acceptance.

2. Next likely is that they will listen to it politely and then ignore it.

3. Finally, they may listen to it, become perturbed if not angry, but not communicate this directly.

We have a tendency to adjust to the ways of thinking of the superior. You find yourself telling him what he wants to hear—or if you cannot, you try to do it in the way you think he wants to hear it. Often an embassy can be split on major issues. The ambassadors do not deal with the issues. If a low Foreign Service officer makes a way-out point, he can be ignored. If a senior Foreign Service officer does the same, he also can be ignored, but he also runs the risk of being moved out.

UNDERUTILIZATION OF CAPABILITIES

I was given a job to type 3,000 file cards after I had been told in my orientation how much the Foreign Service valued initiative. I was furious. Why not use a girl for this? I asked and was told that secretaries were scarce. I thought, if they'd get rid of some of the excess officers they might afford secretaries.

Anyway, I started typing. But I decided to research the job on my own. I found out:

1. Another Foreign Service officer had done the same thing one year ago.

2. The process was so slow that by the time I finished the last one, the first one would be obsolete.

I came up with a simple solution and took it to my boss. He told me that was a great idea but it wouldn't work. When I asked him why, he gave me a vague reason. I felt that either he didn't want to bother with developing the idea, or that he didn't want to admit to a superior that a junior man thought this out. He told me to go back to my typing.

I continued my typing so that no one would consider me as a troublemaker. But I wrote up the plan as a beneficial suggestion. Nothing happened. I decided finally that there was nothing that I could do. So I started asking around. First thing I found out was how many people had experienced the same kind of thing. "Join the club." I was taught to complain about my job to certain people but not be too obvious about it. Finally, I got out. One good thing I learned was how to beat the system.

Many of my friends have had similar experiences. This was a shock to me. I took a $2,000 cut to join the Foreign Service. When I went to someone more senior than I to complain, he too began by telling me of the clerical shortage. He also cautioned me not to rock the boat.

One thing people don't realize upstairs is the bind you feel with a dull job. They tell you during orientation to strive to live up to the Foreign Service image of initiative, action, etc. If you accept a dull job then you are not meeting the image. If you do not accept it, you can be viewed as a troublemaker.

CRISIS ORIENTATION AND OVERSTAFFING

I believe that we staff for crises. Once the crisis is over it is hard to cut back. In the organization from which I came, we had three Foreign Service officers doing one-third of the work, rather than one who could do it all easily. But that's bureaucracy.

41

Overstaffing is one of the major problems around here. I guess this is an inherent bureaucratic phenomenon—you know, Parkinson's law.

Researcher: You seem resigned to this.

Respondent: Yes, what the hell is there to do?

Researcher: Before you said people work long hours. Now you mention there are many more people available than are necessary; why then do people work long hours?

Respondent: I've often wondered about that. Sometimes I think all of us are so starved to do something important that we stick around hoping that it will come up.

Another respondent: Sometimes, I do not want to go home because others are working.

Another respondent: One senior man told me that this is one of the perplexing questions. You work hard and long and when you get home you don't know what you have accomplished.

Previous respondent: I see this during a crisis. When we had one in ——, I was duty officer. What impressed me was the number of people who came around even though they had nothing to do with the crisis.

———————

We create and enjoy crises. Our office operates with crises.

Why? I don't know. I wish I knew. But all of us like them. I know I enjoy them.

Sometimes I think that the reason that we create crises is that there are too many people for everyday work and they have little to do. The more the crises, the better they like it. They feel like they're doing something.

There is a sense of elation that comes with a crisis.

We're responsive to a name on a memo. The more important the names, the bigger the crises.

PROMOTIONS

Promotions depend on the superior. If you get along with him, he will fill out a good report.

Sometimes promotions also depend on whether or not the superior knows how to write a good recommendation.

It used to be that they would show you all the rating. Then they stopped that with the hope that the superior would be free to be frank. Now they let you see half of it—that's a farce.

Thus we find that the senior and junior Foreign Service officers seem to agree with each other on some of the crucial problems of the internal organization of the State Department.

* * * * *

In closing, I want to emphasize the point made at the outset. This analysis is only partial. It focuses primarily on the causes of problems and says very little about the sources of strengths, especially the professional competence and the personal commitment of the participants. The State Department is not about to collapse, thanks to the excellence of its people.

However, I do not want to gloss over the implications of the analysis. The State Department as an organization may not collapse, but it has, in my opinion, the seeds for its own rigidity, sluggishness, and pathology. I have no precise measure of how deeply the State Department is strangled by the forces described above. I feel confident that the stranglehold is not so strong as to make change impossible. I also feel confident that, whatever the state of affairs is found to be today, things will get worse rather than better unless positive steps are taken.

I believe the Foreign Service personnel are capable of, indeed are desirous of, facing reality and turning their organization about so that it can build upon the capacities of its members and achieve its mission with greater effectiveness.

4

Recommendations

I began the report with the Secretary's concern that individuals within the State Department were apparently not willing to assume and, when appropriate, enlarge their responsibility. I hope I have shown that these people may have ample reason to hesitate to assume or enlarge their responsibility. Many who have the desire and the competence to take risks and enlarge their responsibility may not do so because they are embedded in a living system (i.e., <u>the actual behavior and attitudes of the participants</u>) that does not tend to reward such behavior. Until the living system is altered it is premature to blame these difficulties upon the individual members. If the living system is altered so that it does reward risk-taking and initiative, and if individuals still hesitate to behave in these ways, then we would begin to have evidence that this problem is primarily one of individuals who fear taking initiative and not the system suppressing their initiative.

<u>Recommendation I.</u>   A long-range change program should be defined with the target being to change the living system of the State Department.

Living systems cannot be changed by drawing new organizational charts or by speeches from the top deploring the lack of initiative. The former strategy, although important, misses the initial problem: namely, that of unfreezing the behavior and values of the participants.   The latter strategy tends to be perceived by subordinates as punishing, or at a minimum, off the mark, because they believe they are ready to take the initiative if the system permitted them to do so.

The first step in changing a living system is to help the participants become aware of the degree to which their everyday behavior and attitudes conform to those aspects of the system that cause ineffectiveness. This initial step cannot be overemphasized. It may be difficult for the reader to believe, but it is nevertheless true that the most heavily documented conclusion in this analysis (and in the analyses made of business, university, and religious and health organizations) is the lack of awareness by the supervisory members of the degree to which their present behavior and attitudes cause some of the very problems that they abhor. That such an awareness can be developed has been demonstrated at the Airlie House conferences and continued in subsequent conferences such as those held at the Tidewater Inn.

The second step is to help the individuals, working with the people with whom they naturally and most frequently interact, to change their behavior and attitudes. The recent program with the Deputy Under Secretary of State and his executive group and the beginning program of the Assistant Secretary of State for African Affairs provide concrete illustrations that such change in behavior and attitudes is possible and that it has important payoffs for organizational development.

Changing behavior and attitudes can be accomplished in many ways. The method being recommended here is to change that behavior and those attitudes which are alterable by changing the nature of the relationships among people. Individually oriented therapeutic changes are not being recommended. A fundamental assumption of the approach being recommended is that the participants are internally unconflicted to the point that they can learn from each other, if the living system will permit them to shed the social, normal, everyday defenses and masks. This assumption has been strongly supported by the experiences to date.

Recommendation II. The first stage of the change program should focus on the behavior and leadership style of the most senior participants within the Department of State.

Experience in organizational development programs suggests that it makes little sense—indeed it could be disastrous—for the lower levels to attempt to change, only to find that their superiors are not aware of the extent to which their (the superiors') behavior and attitudes are important causes of system ineffectiveness. No data were uncovered to lead us to believe that the upper levels were more competent in dealing with substantive or administrative issues that threatened people, or that they were less blind to their impact upon others. Indeed, from the illustrations obtained during the conferences, and if we extrapolate from studies in comparable living systems, the indication is that the top superiors are probably heavily involved in creating the system's norms that lead to difficulties. The top officers of the State Department, therefore, have the responsibility of taking the initiative in beginning to explore the impact that they have upon the living system and therefore upon the individuals working within the system.

Recommendation III. Simultaneously with the involvement of the top, similar change activities should be initiated in any subpart which shows signs of being ready to change.

Several regional bureaus, several functional groups, and more embassies than can be helped (because of lack of trained staff) have asked for assistance in organizational development. There is, therefore, a felt need at key points for change. This should be followed up as soon as the availability of competent help permits. Whenever possible, subunits should be selected that are in organic relationship to each other (e.g., embassies in South America; the appropriate country directors; the top group of ARA, including the Assistant Secretary of State).

Recommendation IV. The processes of organizational change and development that are created should require the same behavior and attitudes as those we wish to inculcate into the system.

If we are seeking to encourage Foreign Service employees to take more initiative, enlarge their responsibility, take risks, then the processes of organizational change and development should provide, by design, opportunities to test and experience these new behaviors. Too often organizations mount expensive programs to increase employee initiative, which are centrally controlled and executed. The result of this is that the employees feel manipulated, unilaterally directed, their responsibility for change restricted, and their propensity for risk-taking suppressed. The resulting discrepancy between the top administrators' pronouncements and the employees' experiences during the change program leads to frustration and resentment, which, in turn, does not lead to an internal commitment to change.

This does not mean that programs cannot be designed and that specialists in organizational development should not be used. It means that the consultants should be used primarily to help the line officers acquire the new skills and develop the new designs that are necessary if the change program is to be effective. The line administrators of the State Department should be in control of the pace and direction of the program and not the consultants (whether they come from within or without the organization).

The Department of State has already developed a change program which has many of the characteristics of an effective program for organizational development. The program is called Action for Organizational Development (ACORD). ACORD could easily become the foundation for self-renewal of the living system in the State Department. If this does become the case, then the ACORD staff must make clear to the others within the State Department their objectives regarding strategy for change. There is, unfortunately, a misunderstanding among officers outside the O area, a belief that ACORD is an O program. According to my observations, nothing is further from the desires of those who are connected with ACORD. The ACORD staff prefer to act as consultants to line administrators of units that wish to develop themselves. As a result of their reeducation, they realize that the door to a particular unit's development is locked to, and can only be opened by, those who are members of that system.

In this connection, it is important to point out the underlying similarities between the basic assumptions of an effective organizational development program and the Planning, Programming and Budgeting System (PPBS). Both assume that an organization should be able to generate and bring to bear upon a problem all the relevant information and to do so in time so that it is useful to those trying to solve problems and make decisions. A relatively closed living system will produce a rigid, incomplete, and ineffective PPBS program because it cannot generate the valid data, nor could it integrate these data if they were to become available.

The computer, in short, is like a magnifying mirror. It will reflect, in bold images, the true nature of the human system. It cannot do anything else, for it cannot reach heights that have not been reached by its human programmers.

Recommendation V. As the organizational development activities produce a higher level of leadership skills and begin to reduce the system's defenses in the area of interpersonal relations, the participants should be helped to begin to reexamine some of the formal policies and activities of the State Department that presently may act as inhibitors to organizational effectiveness. The reexamination should be

48

conducted under the direction of line executives with the help of inside or outside consultants.

Change in behavior and values will be neither effective nor long lasting if other aspects of the living system are not also changed with an eye to making them congruent with the overall change desired. Trust and openness, expansion of initiative and risk-taking cannot last long in a system where formal policies inhibit their expression. Three important areas that require close reexamination, under the direction of the line executives, are:*

(1) The processes by which Foreign Service employees are evaluated and rated. Our respondents clearly felt that weaknesses existed in the formal procedures, the forms, and above all in the human relationships between a superior and a subordinate during the period when the latter was being rated and the rating discussed with him. The participants especially emphasized that much more attention needed to be given to the quality of the dialog between the rating officer and the rated officer.

(2) The processes of promotion also need to be reexamined. Respondents felt that promotion too often depended upon the ability of impersonal panels to reach valid comparative judgments about personnel, based on written records. Considerable doubt was expressed that the system worked effectively. However, the respondents were unable to develop new promotion processes that might be more effective. This is not surprising since there was very little objective data on the actual method of operation of this very complicated promotion process.

(3) The inspection processes should be reexamined to make them more useful to the ambassador. The inspection process should become less an efficiency report and more a process by which the top field officers are helped to diagnose the effectiveness of their units and to plan new programs and activities to increase that effectiveness.** Much research exists in universities and much experience exists in large corporations as to how the inspection processes could be modified to become processes of individual and organizational development.

---

*Unfortunately, my data do not permit me to be more concrete in recommending specific changes. Much research is needed in these activities to generate needed valid data from which informal decisions can be made.
**The most recent inspection teams have already attempted several positive changes in this direction.

49

Recommendation VI. The similarities and interdependencies between administration and substance need to be made more explicit and more widely accepted.

The field of administration in universities as an academic discipline has changed, and is continuing to change, radically. Much of what was previously included in the concept of administration has been rejected as not having intellectual content worthy of the university level. The old concept of administration has been given new meaning and content. It has been filled with concepts derived from empirical research and tested theories in the social sciences, applied mathematics, statistics, electrical engineering, and information sciences. As the content has been altered, the gap between administration as a curriculum and the curriculum in the arts and sciences has also been narrowed. Today, in the top universities, these fields are fully integrated in the arts and sciences faculties. Also, the intellectual quality of the students taking, and the faculty teaching, the courses in the administrative sciences has increased sharply.

I believe the same process of integration is necessary between the substantive and administrative activities in the State Department. Any system that differentiates and then separates its administrative from its substantive processes dooms itself to difficulties. There is much evidence from research in hospitals, research organizations, and universities that if the administrative processes are second-class activities, the total system, including the substantive activities, will eventually become rigid and ineffective. Second-class administrative processes attract second-class people, who, given their lower status and fewer resources, produce poor quality administration. This, in turn, begins to influence negatively the activities of the substantive side. Soon the substantive employee, be he a doctor, professor, or political officer, will find himself spending precious time extricating himself from seemingly senseless administrative red tape.

Many of the top administrative personnel and substantive officers of the State Department recognize these problems. The new program for organizational development can become the vehicle by which these two processes can be more effectively integrated.

Recommendation VII. The State Department's internal capacity in the new areas of behavioral-science-based knowledge should be increased immediately.

The Department of State should develop a small but highly competent and senior consultant group that can operate at all levels. Also, younger men might be attracted at the lower levels to this new career of agents of system development and renewal. Finally, cooperative arrangements might be developed with appropriate universities to develop a crash program to train consultants from among substantive officers who are in mid-career and who desire such education.

Another important step is for the Foreign Service Institute to increase the proportion of its curriculum devoted to these new areas. This would help to educate all Foreign Service personnel to the new concepts.

Recommendation VIII. A long-range research program should be developed, exploring the possible value of the behavioral disciplines to the conduct of diplomacy.

The new concepts of behavioral science include principles concerning the effective influence of individual, group, inter-group, and organizational behavior. Thus far, in all the organizations studied, when administration and substance had been separated, the members of the latter never felt the principles utilized by the former group could apply to them. However, in all cases where an integration has been attempted, the opposite turned out to be the case.

A long-range research program is needed on the possible value of behavioral science knowledge on the conduct of diplomacy. For example, individuals who screen out behavior unknowingly, as the officers did who were described in this report, may screen out behavior when they are interacting with individuals representing foreign nations. It frequently occurred in our small group meetings that one ambassador felt certain that he was hiding his anger. However, the rest of the group experienced him as angry but did not tell him so. If this can occur with individuals of one's own organization and within the same culture, may it not occur even more easily and in a more complicated manner with foreign representatives? Another example was given by many middle and younger officers who felt that they had to learn to write official documents whose tenor fitted with the defenses of their boss. They reported that the resulting language was not as clear as they felt it could be.

Turning to groups, I have been able to observe briefing sessions which were handled in such a way as to magnify the relationship between the United States and the country involved. There is much research and knowledge about the most effective processes to be used when a team is being briefed about an adversary so that one minimizes unrealized screening. Also,

I have observed intergroup rivalries within the State Department either ignored until the last possible moment or resolved in ways that helped to encourage the loser to have feelings of "I'll not lose again," and the winner to feel a hero. Such win-lose dynamics can play havoc with the problem-solving effectiveness of a system that depends upon the inputs of many units with different views and interests.

Examples were cited by the individuals in which, because of poor communication within an embassy and/or between an embassy and Washington, a cable was sent to Washington that did not represent the judgment of the Foreign Service officers involved in the problem.

* * * * *

Let me repeat again that these problems are not unique to the State Department. All systems, including universities, seem to be plagued with them. The encouraging trends, however, are (1) that top executives are interested in reducing these problems in the interests of long-range organizational health, and (2) that knowledge is being generated that can be of immediate and long-range assistance in this challenge.

Let me also repeat that this report differs significantly from others which have been critical of the Department of State, in that it fundamentally asserts that there is a capability within the Foreign Service community to change the living system and to be in control of its organizational destiny. The basic steps toward organizational development are the courage and capacity to face reality squarely. I believe that anyone who reads the analyses in this report (which were made by Foreign Service officers) must conclude, as I have, that the Foreign Service has more than met this important challenge.

www.ingramcontent.com/pod-product-compliance
Lightning Source LLC
Chambersburg PA
CBHW022132280326
41933CB00007B/653